START-UP SCIENCE

Floating and Sinking

By Jack Challoner

Contents

Floating and Sinking 3
Things that Float 4
Things that Sink 6
Objects in Water 8
Boats and Rafts 10
Big Ships 12
Living in Water 14
Whales and Sharks 16
Underwater 18
The Ocean 20
Hot Air 22
Balloons and Airships 24
In the Pond 26
Floating Liquids 28
Floating and Swimming 30
Glossary and Index 32

RSVP
**RAINTREE
STECK-VAUGHN**
P U B L I S H E R S
The Steck-Vaughn Company

Austin, Texas

Published by Raintree Steck-Vaughn Publishers, an imprint of
Steck-Vaughn Company

Editors: Kim Merlino, Kathy DeVico
Project Manager: Lyda Guz
Electronic Production: Scott Melcer

Photo Credits: cover: Robert Harding Picture Library: top;
NHPA: bottom Henry Ausloos;
Bubbles: p. 31 Ian West;
Collections: p. 8 Anthea Sieveking;
FLPA: p. 4 W. Wisniewski; p. 26 H. Eisenbeiss;
Robert Harding Picture Library: pp. 12, 15, 22;
NHPA: p. 6 Jeff Goodman; p. 10 Martin Harvey; p. 14 Lutra;
p. 16 Henry Ausloos; p. 17 Gerard Lacz; p. 18 Norbert Wu;
p. 20 David E. Myers; p. 23 Nigel J. Dennis; p. 27 David Woodfall;
Planet Earth Pictures: p. 3 Doug Perrine; pp. 9, 28 Flip Schulke;
Tony Stone Images: p. 13; TRH/U.S. Navy: p. 25.

All other photographs by Claire Paxton.

Library of Congress Cataloging-in-Publication Data

Challoner, Jack.
Floating and sinking / by Jack Challoner.
p.   cm. — (Start-up science)
Includes index.
ISBN 0-8172-4317-8 (hardcover)
1. Floating bodies — Experiments — Juvenile literature.
1. Archemedes' principle — Experiments — Juvenile literature.
[1. Floating bodies — Experiments.   2. Archmedes' priniciple —
Experiments.   3. Experiments.]   I. Title   II. Series: Challoner, Jack.
Start-up science.
QC147.5.C48   1997
532'.2—dc20
95-40152
CIP
AC

Printed in Spain
Bound in the United States
1 2 3 4 5 6 7 8 9 0 LB 99 98 97 96

Floating and Sinking

This book will answer lots of questions that you may have about floating and sinking. But it will also make you think for yourself.

Each time you turn a page, you will find an activity that you can do yourself at home or at school. You may need help from an adult.

Why does a block of metal sink, while wood floats? How do huge metal ships float? Have you ever wondered why fish do not sink?

Things that Float

What materials do you know that float in water? Some plastics float in water, and most types of wood do, too. Materials that float are said to be **buoyant**.

Moving logs

These logs have been cut from huge trees. The best way to move a large number of logs is to float them down a river.

Did you know?

A block of wood weighs less than a block of metal that is the same size.

Floating materials

Some materials always float in water. The materials in this bowl are cork, polystyrene, rubber, and wax.

Now try this

Most people think that heavy things sink, and light things float. Is this always true?

You will need:

a light metal coin,
a heavy wooden block,
a bowl of water

1. Hold the coin in one hand and the block in the other. Which one feels heavier?

2. Put the coin and the wood into the bowl of water. Does the heavier one sink?

Things that Sink

Anything that is heavier than the same amount of water will sink in water. Some ocean creatures sink in water. They live on the ocean bottom.

On the ocean floor

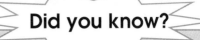

Most animals that live in the ocean can float or swim to the surface if they need to.

Others, like this clam, stay on the bottom because they cannot float.

Sinking materials

Some materials sink in water. The materials in this bowl are chalk, modeling clay, steel, and glass.

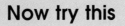

Now try this

Will two different objects of the same size and shape both sink or both float? Find out for yourself.

You will need:
a small block of wood,
modeling clay,
a bowl of water

1. Use the modeling clay to make a block that is the same shape and size as the wood.

2. Put the two blocks in the bowl of water. Which one sinks?

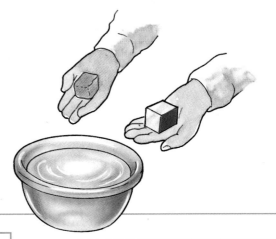

Objects in Water

Objects seem to weigh less when they are in water. This is because the water supports them. Putting objects in water pushes the water aside.

Water support

Floating in water can help people with injuries. The water supports the body, so that the body isn't pushing on the injured part as much.

Did you know?

When you take a bath, your body pushes the water out of the way. If the tub is too full, it overflows.

Lightweight

This diver can lift the heavy pot because of the support the water gives. Once it is out of the water, the pot will feel much heavier.

Now try this

You can see the support that water gives, as it pushes up on anything that you put into it.

You will need:
modeling clay, a rubber band, a bowl of water

1. Break the rubber band in one place to make one long strip. Tie it around the modeling clay.

2. Hold the free end of the rubber band, so that the modeling clay hangs from it. See how the weight stretches the rubber band.

3. Hang the modeling clay in the water. Is the rubber band as long as it was before?

Boats and Rafts

A boat floats because it has a large base. The water pushes up on the bottom of the boat, making it float.

Wooden raft

This hovercraft does not float on water. It hovers over the surface, because it is lifted by a cushion of air.

For thousands of years, people have used rafts like this one to float on water.

Rafts are usually made of wood and can travel great distances.

Full of air

This boy is paddling a kayak. The kayak has air in it, which helps it to float. No water can get into the kayak. Can you see why?

Now try this

A material that usually sinks can be made to float, by making it into a boat shape.

You will need:
modeling clay, a bowl of water

1. Roll some clay into a ball.

2. Put the ball into the water. Does it sink or float?

3. Flatten out another piece of clay, and turn up the edges so that it looks like a boat.

4. Put the boat shape into the water. Does it sink or float?

Big Ships

Most big ships are made of steel. Steel is a metal that does not usually float in water. But if it is made into the shape of a boat, it can float easily and even carry a load.

Did you know?

All big ships were made of wood until about 150 years ago. This paddle steamer was one of the first steel ships ever made.

Balanced load

A ship's load is called its **cargo**. If all of the cargo is on one side of the ship, the ship will tilt and may roll over. This crane is being used to load the cargo evenly.

Too heavy?

The more cargo a ship is carrying, the lower the ship floats in the water. Lines on the side of the ship show how low the ship is floating.

Now try this

A boat shape can float with a load in it. But if there is too much weight, it will sink.

You will need:
a clean, empty plastic container, a bowl or tub of water, marbles

1. Float the plastic container in the tub of water.

2. Put a few marbles in it. The container will float a little lower.

3. How many marbles does it take to make the container sink?

Living in Water

There are many different types of fish, and all of them live in water. To do this, they must not be too buoyant, or they will float to the top. But they must not sink either.

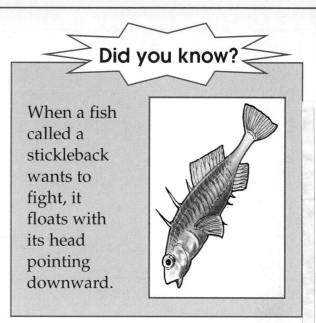
How do fish float?

Most fish have a small bag of air called a **swim bladder** inside their bodies. This helps fish to control how bouyant they are in the water.

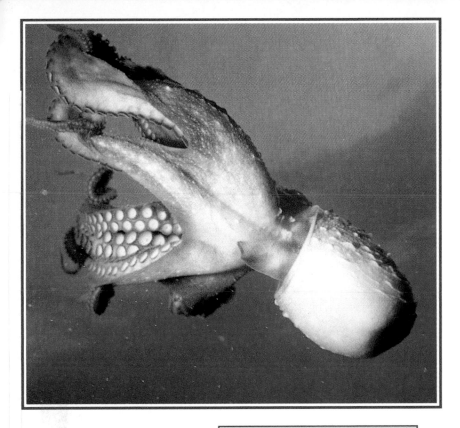

Not a fish

An octopus lives in water, but it is not a fish. It is a type of animal called a **mollusk**. Long ago, people thought that large octopuses were sea monsters.

Now try this

You can find out how a fish's swim bladder works.

You will need:
a small balloon, a plastic tube, a rubber band, a tub of water, modeling clay

1. Push the neck of the balloon over one end of the tube. Hold it in place with the rubber band.

2. Wrap a large lump of clay around the neck of the balloon. Use enough to make the end of the tube sink in the tub of water.

3. Now, blow and suck gently into the other end of the tube.

What causes the balloon to float? What causes it to sink?

Whales and Sharks

Sharks and whales both live in water. Sharks are large fish, but whales are not fish. They are **mammals**. Whales have to come to the surface of the water to breathe air.

Sinking shark

A shark does not have a swim bladder, like other fish. If it stops swimming, it slowly sinks to the bottom.

Did you know?

Some whales stay underwater for as long as an hour and a half without coming up for air.

Fast swimmer

A dolphin is a type of whale with a long, thin body. This helps it to move quickly through the water.

Now try this

Whales' bodies are mostly water. This is why they do not float to the top or sink to the bottom.

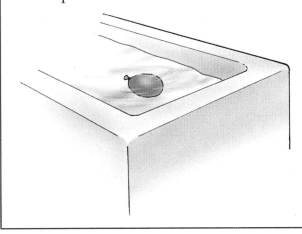

You will need:
a balloon,
a tub of water

1. Ask an adult to fill the balloon with water, so that it is about half its full size. Ask the adult to tie the neck of the balloon.

2. Now put the balloon in the water. It will only just float, or only just sink.

Underwater

Submarines are used to explore the oceans. They can become buoyant so that they float to the top of the water. They can also be made less buoyant so that they sink.

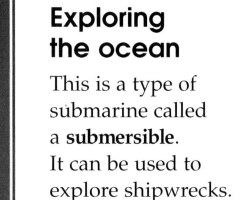

Exploring the ocean

This is a type of submarine called a **submersible**. It can be used to explore shipwrecks.

Did you know?

Submarines have traveled all the way around the world underwater without coming to the surface at all.

Submarine raisins

Small bubbles of gas in this fizzy drink make these raisins buoyant. The raisins float, but once they reach the surface, the bubbles burst. Then the raisins sink again.

Now try this

You can make your own submarine, which will float or sink as you wish.

You will need:
a used wooden match,
modeling clay,
a plastic bottle,
a bowl of water

1. Put a tiny bit of modeling clay onto one end of the match — enough to make it float upright.

2. Fill the bottle right to the top, and put the match into it. Screw the top on tightly.

3. If you squeeze the bottle, the match should sink. When you let go, the match will float again.

The Ocean

All sorts of things can be found floating in the ocean or washing up on the beach. The ocean is salty, and things float better in salty water.

Floating ice

In some very cold parts of the world, large chunks of ice, called **icebergs**, float in the ocean. Most of an iceberg is hidden below the surface of the water.

Washed up

Many things from the ocean are washed up on beaches. How do you think they came to be in the ocean?

Now try this

You can see that things float better in saltwater than in freshwater.

You will need:
water, a fresh egg, lots of table salt, a drinking glass

1. Fill the glass with water over a kitchen sink.

2. Gently put the egg into the water. It will not float.

3. Now pour salt into the water, until the egg floats.

Hot Air

Floating does not only happen in water. Hot-air balloons can rise into the air because they contain hot air. Hot air floats on cold air.

Taking off

The air inside hot-air balloons is heated by flames of burning gas. When the air is hot enough, the balloon floats up into the air.

Did you know?

People flying in hang gliders use rising hot air to go higher. Some birds do the same.

Flying high

Where the sun heats up the land, the air above the land becomes hot, too. The hot air floats upward and helps birds, like this vulture, to rise.

Now try this

You can see for yourself that hot air rises.

You will need:
a blow-dryer

1. Ask an adult to turn on the blow-dryer.

2. Stand about 3 feet (1 m) from the blow-dryer. Ask the adult to point the blow-dryer straight at you. Now feel where the hot air goes. Does it rise?

Balloons and Airships

Helium is a gas, like air. Balloons filled with helium float in the air, just like hot-air balloons. Airships are filled with helium, and so are some toy balloons.

Floating balloons

Have you ever held a balloon filled with helium? If you let go of the string, the balloon will float up, and you may lose it.

Did you know?

The first airships used hydrogen gas instead of helium. Hydrogen gas can explode, so some airships blew up.

Air travel

This is an airship. People sit in the cabin underneath the balloon. A motor moves the airship forward.

Now try this

See how difficult it is to get a helium balloon to float in midair.

You will need:

a helium balloon on a string, modeling clay

1. Put enough modeling clay onto the end of the string to make the balloon sink to the ground.

2. Now, take away the modeling clay, bit by bit, until the balloon just floats. See if you can make it stay still in the air.

In the Pond

A pond is a great place to see things floating and sinking. Ducks swim in the water, plants float on the top, and some insects walk on the surface of the water.

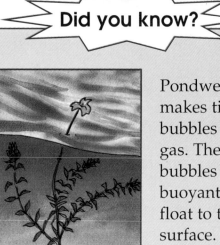
On the surface

This water boatman is not floating on the water. It is walking on the surface of the water. It is so light that the surface of the water supports its weight.

Pond plants

Some plants live in ponds. The leaves of these water lilies float on the surface of the water, so that they can catch sunlight.

Now try this

To show how insects can walk on a pond, make a paper clip stay on the surface of a bowl of water.

You will need:

a paper clip, a few tissues, a bowl of water

1. Fold the tissues, and place the paper clip on top.

2. Now place the tissues gently on the water.

3. After a few seconds, the tissues will sink, but the paper clip will stay on the surface.

Floating Liquids

When people hear the word "floating," they usually think of solid things, like wood.

But liquids can float, too. Water floats on some liquids, but sinks in others.

Oil spill

Large ships are used to carry oil. Sometimes they crash into rocks and spill oil in the water. The oil floats on the water, and it can kill birds, fish, and many other animals.

Did you know?

A liquid like dish washing liquid is sometimes sprayed on an oil spill to help clean it up.

Three liquids

Oil floats on water, but water floats on syrup. Can you tell which of these three liquids is which in this glass?

Hot water

In this photograph, hot water, colored red, is floating to the surface of cold water. This is just like hot air floating on cold air.

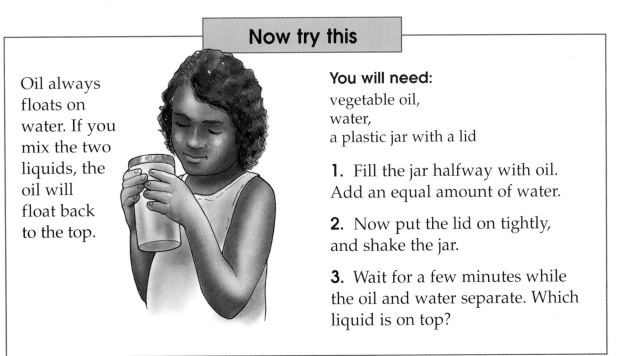

Now try this

Oil always floats on water. If you mix the two liquids, the oil will float back to the top.

You will need:
vegetable oil,
water,
a plastic jar with a lid

1. Fill the jar halfway with oil. Add an equal amount of water.

2. Now put the lid on tightly, and shake the jar.

3. Wait for a few minutes while the oil and water separate. Which liquid is on top?

Floating and Swimming

When you learn to swim, you need something to help you float until you learn how.

Most people learn to swim by using buoyant, air-filled armbands or kickboards.

Learning to swim

This girl is holding onto a kickboard made of a buoyant material called polystyrene. This helps her float while she is learning to swim.

Did you know?

In the Dead Sea, in Israel, people float high in the water. This is because the water is very salty.

Floating on air

The air in this toy makes it very buoyant.
This helps the girl to float.

Now try this

Air makes things buoyant.
See this for yourself.

You will need:
a balloon, a tub or sink filled
with water

Make sure an adult helps
you with this activity.

1. Fill the balloon with air. Tie a
knot in the end to keep the air in.

2. Now try to push the balloon
underwater. The balloon pushes
your hands up.

Glossary

buoyant Able to float

cargo A ship's load

iceberg A block of ice that floats on
the ocean

mammals Animals that feed on their
mother's milk when they are young

mollusk An animal such as an octopus,
snail, or slug

submarine and **submersible** A vehicle
that can travel underwater

swim bladder A buoyant bag of air inside
a fish's body, which helps it to float

Index

airships 24, 25
animals 6

balloons 22, 24–25
boats 10, 11, 12, 13

canoes 11
cargo 12, 13
chalk 7
clams 6
cork 4

Dead Sea 30
dolphins 17
ducks 26

fish 3, 14, 15, 16

glass 7

hang gliders 22
hovercrafts 10

icebergs 20
insects 26

liquids 28–29

metals 3, 4, 5, 6, 7
modeling clay 7
mollusks 15

ocean 6, 18, 20–21
octopuses 15
oil 28–29
oil spills 28

paddle steamers 12
plastic 4
polystyrene 5, 30
ponds 26–27
pondweed 26

rafts 10
rubber 5

salt 20, 21, 30
sea 6, 18, 20–21
sharks 16
ships 3, 12, 13

steel 7, 12
sticklebacks 14
submarines 18, 19
submersibles 18
swim bladder 14, 15, 16
swimming 30–31
syrup 29

vultures 23

water 4–20, 26–31
water boatman 26
wax 4
whales 16, 17
wood 3, 4, 5, 7, 10

© 1995 Belitha Press Ltd.